Sibling Rivalry Press, LLC
159 Sunset Drive
North Little Rock, AR 72118
info@siblingrivalrypress.com
www.siblingrivalrypress.com

ISBN:978-1-943977-86-4
First Sibling Rivalry Press Edition: July 2025

BROTHERFUL

BROTHERFUL

BRYAN BORLAND

SIBLING RIVALRY PRESS

DISTURB/ENRAPTURE

FOR KATE & BRADY,
WHO KNOW.

Lines from Previous Poems

I was a younger brother for thirteen years.

My brother never made it
to this second puberty of silver hair. In my mind
he's a mixture of space and light.

His room felt the way houses do
when their families leave them,
a cold and quiet winter with
the curtains drawn.

After his funeral,
I washed my hands until they bled.

I cannot remember
my brother's voice. The poetry of it
abandons me.

I knew before my parents
my brother was dead.

I couldn't cease being
a thirteen-year-old boy
even on the day we buried him.

My secret weapon
was the blood clot that went
from his leg to his lungs.

I traded his belongings for the attention of undeserving boys.

I pretend his arm is around me.

I still wonder what he'd say, my brother.
I still wonder what he'd say, my brother.
I still wonder what he'd say, my brother.
I still wonder what he'd say, my brother.
I still wonder what he'd say, my brother.
my brother.

SONS OF ABRAHAM

My grief grows with the years. I count
seventeen Octobers come and gone,

imagine a green-eyed boy
with hair the color of straw,

wooden walls sturdy on branches
long since chopped and used

for firewood. The older I get,
the more aches and pains: a nephew

and a treehouse, these things
my brother would have made.

Originally published in *MY LIFE AS ADAM*

POEMS & INSTRUCTION

INSTRUCTION

If your story had a beginning
it would start not with light
and dark but in the color between
call it shadow call it dawn call it just
before morning waking before your father
when you alone in the world hear existence
into existence before sounds had names
when knowledge was only intuition
and soon the smell of coffee and you
floating with no foothold
no gravity everything miraculous
your small body this new planet
of possibility oh intelligent fledging
there's a word for this
you'll learn and forget many times

LINEAGE (FAMILY)

There are things you aren't meant
to understand.

The only brother to survive the war
had twelve children and four generations
later here you are.

Decades ago someone fed a dog
and because of that you have a dog.

You'll never know the woman who
planted the tree but you love her
because she did.

SIBLING RIVALRY

You will age beyond him
in seven years' time, but this thought
hasn't yet occurred to you. Your hair
will autumn to gray; his will remain
the dark of peace, the color
you imagine of space
or Heaven. The purple-
blue bruises on your perpetually
slugged shoulders
will be slow to heal,
but they will heal. You will fade
from your mother's line of vision.
In other moments she will
smother you, warn you against
crossing the gods or the streets.
When people tell you your voice
sounds like his, you will lock your door.
You will ask questions, close your eyes,
and you will hear him answer.
When you open your eyes
you will be an only child.

THEY SAY THE MUSIC YOU HEAR AT
FOURTEEN IS THE MUSIC OF YOUR LIFE

"I want to be a jukebox song"
Jack Veasey, "When I Reincarnate"
(1955-2016)

Small town anywhere a mother is
driving her son to the party
because that's where the boy is
the boy that makes him feel like
a bird just out of the nest part clumsy
wing part maple dream when every
little leap might lead to sky where
each Saturday is its own new
season where the lights will
heartbeat bright and deep
and calf will rise against calf where
a song will begin where he'll open
his mouth to sing instead a
timid moment will bloom to power
first lips like the warm wet mouthpiece
of a trumpet he'll remember
that music every first of his life

SAINT ILLOGIC

Knowing the world is beautiful the spirits
sit in trees along the river watching

us run toward the bend of our inevitable. Seeing
with my real eyes I recognize the ones familiar.

The long-gone poet who writes in birds and thunder.
The maternal grandmother

who loves me more than I know. My brother
visits but rarely as he's a younger sort of forever

leaping through fields of that vast dimension
with a speed I cannot replicate. There he is

twice each year, a hawk or a ladybug.
It's my father who stays within shouting distance.

All his life he was preparing me for something.
All his death, too. He is flickering

lights and music on the radio. Look. I'm not
asking you to believe any of this. The messages

arrive how they arrive—today in the graffiti
fingers of a dark-haired boy. These growing years

gone and I'm beginning to learn his language.
The telephone rings. There is a knock at the door.

If you don't answer,
there is another knock.

We call the dead
and the dead they come.

CARETAKER OF THE WORLD

It is difficult being caretaker of the world.
Last year I wore myself crazy worrying
over every nest in every storm. I can't
stop and move every turtle from every highway
though I try. I dream about the ones I miss. Before I fell
in love with birds, I shot them as boy. Before I fell
in love with birds, I rescued them from stairwells.
I've always been a contradiction of the worst and best
potential. Some call this being human. Some days
I save everything but myself. Some days everything
I save saves me. Some call this being alive.

ELECTRICITY

The beautiful woman tells me that once
a space exists as a place of God it can never lose
that purpose. I believe her. She was talking of a temple
but there's a bedroom down south where a boy gave me
all his angels and they've never left. When people die
in car accidents bouquets of fake flowers grow
by the road to hide the doors that open up
between this life and the next. My grandfather
once kissed my grandmother in a whorehouse
in Carolina. He knew the baby wasn't his but no
one else did and they were married fifty years.
That whorehouse is the church of my family.
I crossed the street this morning where yesterday
another woman danced with something holy in her feet.
Call me crazy I could feel it. She named her god
electric. Tell me we are wrong.

BROTHERS

"The hardest thing I ever did
was coping with the fact, growing up,
that I was in love with my younger brother."
Vytautus Pliura, "Thomas"
(1951-2011)

It wasn't my brother I was in love with,
or even the boys I chose to stand in his shoes,
every one of them, filling their
not-my-brother mouths with
my name, their greedy arms with
trophies from his dying
room. It was the idea of him I was grieving,
or the idea of something like him,
something I didn't yet have
the words to say, that we could have been
closer than we were, that the only time I remember
him touching me was the day the glass cracked
mercury across my face and I broke into the softness
of his hands. I know he must have touched me
more. I know I wanted to be touched, to share
myself with another him, or something like him,
broad but gentle, kin to me, something
like the man I was terrified to be.

THE TALKING NIGHT

There's so much I want to tell you, tell someone.

I stopped talking to my brother when I passed the age he was when he died. I outgrew the him of him, the me to him. Turned off the lights and if I reached my hand into that dark room again I'd pull back something shredded.

I make stories out of death.

He was 21 when he died. We were brothers. We weren't yet friends.

I was a toy delivered in the Christmas of summer when he was seven years old. I think he was intrigued by the idea of me but never quite knew what to make of me.

For the first several years we shared a bedroom. When he moved one room over, I couldn't sleep.

He was the passenger in a car that crossed the center line. Or the other car crossed the center line. I don't guess that's important now. In the photograph on the front page of the newspaper you could see one of his shoes on the shoulder of the road.

I was 13 for many years after he died.

When he moved one room over we shared a wall. My bed was against the wall. I'd press my body to it. That was the only way I could sleep.

He lived ten days after the center line was crossed. Lived long enough to have surgery on his broken leg and for his blood to turn against him.

I've lived my whole life fearing my blood would turn against me, but in a different way.

We weren't yet friends. I'm not sure we would have been.

My friend Kate's brother killed himself. Her sister got a tattoo of their brother's face on her arm. Kate writes poetry about him and worries about her sister's grief. She doesn't understand how the tattoo and the poetry are the same.

I remember the night he moved into the new room. I don't remember any night before then.

If I reach my hand back into that dark room again, I'm not sure whether the something shredded I'd pull back would be me or my brother.

The hospital room was two hours away. The only time I visited, he told me he loved me. He was on pain medication.

Lack of pain is love.

I told Kate if we survive it's because we use our pain in every way we can.

I was a toy delivered in the Christmas of summer. Once he dressed me like a soldier and took me into the woods at night. The dark next to him was thrilling. My back against his back was thrilling.

Once we were where we weren't supposed to be. A friend's house. A rule ignored. An unexpected parent. My brother and I hidden in a closet together. I've already written this metaphor, but when I wrote it, I lied.

Brotherhood at its best is co-conspiracy.

What are the odds of being anyone's brother.

On road trips we'd talk all night in the backseat of the car. Or sometimes in his new room with the door shut and the music on.

The music is still playing.

For a time I was a person in the equation of us. The him of him. The me to him.

My birth changed the equation of his family. His death changed the equation of my family. In each instance something was destroyed and something was created.

What are the odds of being a brother and then not being a brother.

What do I have of his that I still cherish. What do I have of his now that we don't talk.

The morning after I became brotherless, I saw hawks everywhere.

In high school I would tell cute boys sad songs made me think of him. I was trying to get them to kiss me.

Some of them kissed me.

Years after he died I had a dream his entire body was golden.

Years after he died I didn't think of him at all. Not really.

Sad songs made me think of me.

Lack of pain is also pain.

Sometimes I'd knock against the wall we shared. He thought it was just to get a rise out of him but it was for me to know he was there.

Sometimes it feels like we still share a wall. Sometimes I knock against it.

We could have gone one of two ways together. I look at the country now and worry he might have ended up on the other side of something.

Or he could have gone the other way.

I went the way I went without him.

I make stories out of death.

Sometime soon when I'm feeling brave I'll talk to him again. Maybe I'm doing that right now. Maybe I'm having a talking night.

The morning Kate became brotherless, we took her to the airport. When we returned home, there was a hawk in the tree in our front yard.

What are the odds of being anyone's brother.

What are the odds of anything.

WILL

Wondering about the paths these things will
take once I leave for other adventures
the proof of this life picked up along the way or
chosen because they made me think
of someone I loved or a place
the toy robot my brother's that sits on the shelf
not just a material thing the key to unlocking
Christmas morning 1986 when I wasn't brotherless
the red-tailed hawk feather found in the field
when I leave for other adventures
I leave behind my own feathers
my own thousand locked doors
occasionally to be opened by some well-meaning
artist or nephew who doesn't yet exist
but who I already and completely love

ONE GRANDMOTHER

The books are all crooked. I want to straighten them.
I almost wrote fix, but nothing is truly broken.
Nothing in this moment is not how it should be. The smell
of wet dog. The strain on my stubborn eyes. The old friend
reaching out, asking What makes you happy? I answered him
watching the mullein grow from this weather of
uncommon seasons. We lost some limbs last month,
and a corner of the house, but we've made things lovely
again, using the damaged parts to strengthen the rest. I am
my grandmother's grandson. I wish she'd seen this
version of me. I wish we could share a joke, a conversation.
We'd be one dangerous pair. Crooked, someone's project to fix.
The spells I cast all come from her books.

OTHER GRANDMOTHER

I'll miss some details
the vanishing of a dream remembered in pieces
like a past life or old memory
my maternal grandmother
the dark drive to her home on the old country road
the small town big house bigger with her alone
I've dreamed of this house the rooms opening
to rooms familiar as someone else's dream
hallways to other lives immaculate and lonely
but this visit she was alive like my mother
the gaps between them wide as unsaid words
and here in this world I am somehow
a bridge or an extension of hand
this unchanced meeting there wasn't much small talk
a small plate of unremarkable food
but we were family in the ways we could be
we have to understand what's offered is enough

COLLISION

You can't escape ghosts, whether it's Fleetwood Mac
in the coffeeshop or your 8th grade crush at the dive bar
thirty years later. Ghosts might be the wrong word as it implies
a haunting but what if it's more of a welcome caress
or a kiss you think you feel on the back of your neck.
Not that I ever kissed him but god I wanted to. The closest
collision we ever had was when his mother rear-ended
my father as they drove us both to school in the 5th grade.
I cried because it scared me but stopped when he saw
my tears and lied and said I'd hit my head. I doubt he knows
he's a poem in my first book and he'll never know
I'm writing this poem today, but a few years ago
hearing of my publishing success he sent me pages
from his college diary and asked me what I thought. What
I thought was holy shit I'm reading his diary.
The fourteen-year-old version of me still exists.
Another ghost.

SOMETHING SIMPLE

Once, early fishing with the boy who
was like my brother,
our small boat sprung a leak
and began to sink.
One of us paddled
while the other bailed water
with inefficient hands, laughing
at the adventure, our asses wet,
our shirts off and lost to the current
along with things I don't remember. Then
him yelling *snake!*
and me shouting *gator!* when there was
no real danger but the possibility
of danger which meant the possibility of being
anything. When we made it back home
after separate showers we sank
to the bottom of the bed naked together
for the first time like that, all bare and bones
and smelling of soap, too tired to do anything but
fall around the other in pure blue skylight.
In my memories of him it's still that day of night,
of waking dreams, of minutes I fought
to hold still, to stay awake against the boy who
was like my brother, his chest to my back,
and when he breathed, I breathed,
feeling strong and soft and all of seventeen.

THINGS WE FOUND IN NELDA'S SAFE

70 rocks—one for each year
Crow feathers
Laminated recounting of a dream
    wherein her father who died when she was young
    returned and hugged her
Every bird she'd ever seen
534 holy sticks
All the colors of the natural world
Photographs of her family
The telephone number to the Native American music
    program on local public radio
The first rainy morning of autumn
A hawk's wing
Love for her children and grandchildren
Her chocolate fudge recipe
Birdseed
The secrets God told her
Plans for her next life
Paints and beads and sketchbooks and essential oils
2,000 bells
A painting of a willow tree and the actual willow tree
A good amount of marijuana
Various amounts of childlike wonder
A traditional Thanksgiving meal
A Bible
The moon
A buffalo
Everything you ever said to her
Lifestrength
A mirror so we see ourselves in what she loved
Her hair caught in necklace clasps
Her heart
Her laugh

TO OLIVER, NOT YET BORN

Listen, kid. I'm gonna let you in on a secret
I want you to put in your pocket and carry with you
all your life. You are loved.

Before you are even here, you are loved.
This family loves you before we know anything
about you, before we know the color of your hair,
the sound of your voice, or what the weight of you
feels like in our arms. This family loves you.

And this family will love you as much tomorrow
as it does today, in whatever future you arrive in
and exist in. No matter who you become or how
you grow. This family loves you.

This family loves you no matter the choices you'll make,
the clothes you put on your body or what that body
can or cannot do. We'll love you through
wins and losses, good days and bad, mistakes
and disappointments, through every decision
you make, whoever you love or don't, whatever
you make of this life that is wholly and completely
yours. This family loves you.

Put this certainty in your pocket, kid,
or bury it like treasure. The map to it is in
your heart, in your memory, in the face you'll see
in the mirror none of us have seen yet. Return to it
when you need it. Look yourself in the eyes,
whatever color they are and say it like a magic spell
to summon us around you even when we are not there.
Say these words. Say,

I am loved just as I am.

LINEAGE (POETRY)

for Wystan & Frank & Jimmy &
every John in NYC no matter how it's spelled

The New York mothers are held in such high esteem
we forget they were just boy-queens passing cash
between overly dramatic bank accounts. Drinking too
much, gossiping too much, fishing each other's
abandoned drafts out of dumpsters and after-dinner
conversations when bottles were empty and defenses
down. Sometimes they tried too hard to be smart
on the page. Sometimes they were themselves
and those times were the best of times. They thought
themselves above, which was really just survival drag,
a ladder through a window to a party with no invitation.
Then by wit and projection they constructed a door.
We have walked through that door. We have salvaged
their seconds and thirds out of the trash, picked the bones
and made a very fine meal. We too have poured
strong, dropped the names, added color and verb
and stripped facts that wouldn't serve. One August
we bought a house with poetry money
and filled the rooms with stories. Some of them
true. Mothers, you'd be so proud.

12TH VALENTINE'S DAY

I'm wearing red and smell nice in anticipation
of your arrival—how many years and I still chase

butterflies around the room to get it perfect for you.
Sometimes as you walk through

the door I announce all the things I've done
in preparation: the music, the candles, the dishes

clean. You do the same for me sometimes but never
with fanfare. You show. You never tell,

the student who remembers the lessons of how
to write a love poem. I tell to show

with proclamations of good morning and good night.
These are different languages, different paths

to reach the same soft place. Love, we're deep
in conversation. Forgive me if I interrupt;

it's just that I have something important to say.

POWER

I can feel myself softening with age.
I like this place. From here I can watch
flocks of various kinds of birds
rotate around the sky, clock hands
that remind me the season regardless
of the temperamental Arkansas weather.
The biggest thrill yesterday was the arrival
of a giant bag of unshelled peanuts. I'm wooing
the crows like I used to woo boys. No more
hunting knives and twenty-dollar bills
to buy fleeting affection. Crows remember
kind faces for life unlike sweet boys that
grow to be Republican men. I watched
yesterday as workers repaved the road
in front of our house. I worried
briefly about the natural spring that cuts
through the asphalt—the crows'
favorite watering hole. Moments after
the paving I realized I needn't have worried.
The water gained strength and broke through,
already streaming over the street.
Man can't stop what he thinks he can stop.

YOU ARE NOT HERE

I am uncomfortable having this
one-sided conversation.
I dug up your memory
with what appear to be a grown man's hands.
Some days I want to cry.
Some days you've gone to dust.
I am uncomfortable writing the words to fill
your empty grave. These days
I'm the man you never were.
In one version of the past, I am
in our parents' bed. Our mother gives
me a valium as I read the poem
in a condolence card:

Do not stand by my grave and weep.
I am not there, I do not sleep—

I can pinpoint the first time
poetry broke my heart.

THE WILD

with Seth Pennington

Crashing against the mountain, the sun
breaks into a million rubies across the frosted panes
of leaves, and every roof of every house is painted
in a thin wainscoting of frost so the shingles brown
what is underneath. The earth is trying to cure grief
by way of cold and light. I decide it's better to come than
cry. In bedsheets, we are gravel thrown
from the wheels of a pickup; we are making a mess
of our bodies, so our lives will be less so.
In the end, it is snow across your stomach,
raw snow inside you, and I wonder how quickly
the roofs will shed their white morning,
how a window without the sun breaking across it
is just another window, and I think here is love,
when a thing holds within all it can ever be and then
all its nothingness, right after, and the man you were
just inside isn't reaching for his keys, he's spinning
your grandmother's golden wedding ring,
the heirloom you gave him two thousand miles
away in a sudden blizzard, when neither of you had
ever seen snow.

- SP

Now we've seen the world or dreamed it
together   we've named every beast
every bird is familiar   every hole is marked
with the memory of a once-twisted ankle
so we walk our world deliberate   there
is nothing dangerous anymore   if danger
is how we define the beginnings of love   when we
abandon the blueprint of our own possibility
and the pathways into another's body become
the only map that matters   we've memorized
the edges and corners   can follow the other
in the safe of our dark   enough
years have passed that we've been dreaming
of danger again   those individual desires
we buried but never forgot where
you stand on a mountain today
I sit at my desk   we are
thinking of each other   this
is the middle part of love.

- BB

My Papa spent his whole life watching.
He built houses, the blueprint
in his mind, wired strip malls and paper mills
with electric. Drove his wife into Appalachia
to see her glow with gossip
at her sister's side. Now it's all shadows,
the million muted colors dark makes
as his eyes flame out. He gets led through
the home he built by a string,
and in the grocery, he follows the bleached
bright shoes of Grandma shuffling
after cereal and a loaf of honey wheat.
Sometimes you can hear him calling
out after her, when she's moved too fast
down the aisle, and I swear, if I close my eyes
I can hear me in his voice.

- SP

See? There is still danger
though we dare not speak it   we survive
the strange month when everyone dies
the moonflowers bloom one final time
in the approach to a change of season   after you
bury your mother's dog by hand
your mouth is a tomb I stand outside
some goodbyes we see coming like a storm
on the radar and we prepare
some surprise us with a tear in the roof
and rivers falling all over the living
room   we make our plans
our instructions clear   one of us will
drive the car   the other will be
gone   a song will play on the radio
we sang together   there is still danger yes
but we dare not speak it now

                                        - BB

Why does it feel safer to mourn an animal?
We don't speak our own danger,
but I write it and worry I'll be like the poet
who wrote his twin's life ending until it did.
That I'll be left navigating
a life alone with everything
reminding me of you—the books
stamped with our names,
how we mapped our years
in letters scrawled on the insides
of covers so we could trace back
our steps to the love
we found once in the bed in the burgundy
and blue room in the sunrise
when what we knew most was my brokenness,
how every other pair of arms felt like emptiness;
or maybe, even simpler: the beard shavings,
brown and those you say you earned,
the grays that catch so much light, catch
the eye like a star shooting, scattered
at the sink which will crumble me
at the mirror every morning and every night
where I will hate to brush my teeth
like I've always hated to brush my teeth, but in that room
I'll hear you telling me, *Take care of yourself.*

- SP

Those early Sundays having the luxury
of just us   having come into one another's
orbit   sweeping everything else away
work suffered   plants went unwatered
sleep deprived   in a sexual trance
leaner wallets   we spent like no tomorrow
there was no tomorrow   our heaven was this
older now   having grown this universe
you in bed reading in the other room
I watch the lights on the bluffs replaced
by the waking sun   in the house we picked
up where others left off   the for-sale sign
swinging in the front yard then gone
these cabinets that open doors to
the nonlinear notion of time   some days
it's still the day we first touch   the smell of coffee
on your shirt   some mornings
we don't say much at all   I unpack
the boxes   put the book on the shelf
the gift in which you wrote to me
years from now can you still feel the excitement?
and in an autumn then unimaginable
I answer you *yes*.

- BB

I CARVED HIS NAME
INTO THE BARK OF A TREE

and I still remember Ricky's birthday:
45 today & 30 years ago he turned 15
standing on my bloody, needy heart. He loved
me back in all the ways he could & I loved
him until I learned better. I've long known
I wasn't a victim. I was a trap. Sometimes
I wish I would have tried to save him but
I was just a kid. What did I know
other than ache & injury & numbness
& all the things we did to feel
& the taste of dirt & stars & spit
& how together these things built
us into men & how together we learned
& learned & learned & learned
until we learned how to be
alive & alive & alive &
apart.

--

afterthought apart

[44 myself and I would more & only
carve a tree into my own skin
than carve a name into the skin
of a tree & this & this & this
is how we change.]

PLANT DADDIES

It's not what God wants for you, she says,
and she is sincere, and she is sincere when she says
she doesn't see joy in us, though she is speaking
generally, the collective us, though she doesn't know us
beyond the words she hangs from our necks like stones.
Beyond the ways she drowns us in the holy rivers of her mind
but can't fathom how we rise, how we rise. I could
explain to her, but I don't try, the ways joy manifests
in our lives since we removed those stones and replaced them
with each other, with sunflowers that bloom from the deepest
parts of ourselves, with the way he removes his clothes
and puts on my body like the softest glove, and how,
when he tends to me I reach for something to steady myself and
I find the hand of God. I could tell her how he holds me when
I fear I've let him down, or when I actually have, and how
he touches the parts of myself that once carried shame,
meaning he touches all of me and now there is no shame.
Instead, I've turned garden. I grow joy. A whole
garden of joy. Beautiful joy. Queer joy.
Human Joy. God joy.
I am joy.

TURBULENCE

for Loria, on the loss of your brother

Life, or the end of it for a friend, interrupted
my writing this week. They say this is part

of getting older. Do you get used to the deaths
of friends and family? In the blessed gaps

between, you might be mistaken and think
so. I've never grown accustomed to turbulence

no matter how much I fly, even when the captain
says to expect it. That falling feeling, that sudden

drop is, for a time,
the end of time.

SEPTEMBER 11

Not sure really what this date
is supposed to mean   the sharing
of photos   the falling man always falling
the fallen people in mausoleum
a pause   a moment of nothing   they say
let's remember that day   go back to
who we were but I remember blind
hate and unquestioning loyalty
I remember unnecessary war
and the winding tunnels beneath
this country   those twisted roads
we took to get here   I remember
before and after
with us or against us
I remember
against us

LINEAGE (KISSES)

Bryan –

"I have the kiss of Walt Whitman still on my lips,"
Oscar Wilde wrote in a letter to George Ives from
America, 1882. Ives was a pioneering homosexual
emancipationist, the founder of the secret gay society
The Order of Chaeronea. I cannot trace Walt's
kiss through Oscar but rather through another gay
emancipationist (& poet) Edward Carpenter. Carpenter
visited Walt twice, in 1877 & 1884, so bracketing
Oscar's visit. Carpenter & Whitman were intimate as
Carpenter revealed to his American friend & disciple
Gavin Arthur. Gavin was the grandson of President
Chester Arthur. He wrote an interesting book *The
Circle of Sex*, one of the first treatments of alternative
sexualities. Gavin Arthur in later life got to know
that charismatic hipster Neal Cassady who was pretty
much up for kisses & then some with women & men.
Cassady of course became the much-celebrated buddy &
sometimes bed partner of Allen Ginsberg. Allen kissed
Jamie Perry at least once ("Ah! Young punks studying
the Cabala!"). And I had many a kiss from Jamie. Over
to you my dear!

> – Ian [Young, who once kissed me on the lips
> on the Chelsea High Line and said, "This is
> from Walt Whitman!"]

MEDITATING

The quieting of the mind, that meaningless chatter,
the thunderous approaching herd of worries
not yet birthed to body: how many days
does the dog have left, how many do we,
does the boy I wronged still think of me?
Do I kiss my husband enough? Do I make him feel
wanted? Do I make the spirits ashamed when I perform
beneath myself—but quiet all of this & focus
on the breath, the breathing, the space between
the ex & in, & if I need to think of something,
think of stacks of books around me, Bach & family
photographs come to movement & memory,
think of winter blooms & telling friends
how proud I am of them, yes, go by name:
Alana, Lucy, Gustavo, & Guy. Bless
the slow dance to prayer, for my mother, for any
mother, for the woman who wears a blanket
& how she reappears. For the world. Bless
the sounds, don't tune them out, welcome them, hear
the symphony of being. Of imperfection.
Bless the snags in the fabric, bless sick days
that slow me down. Bless the bad day
at one job that makes me work to find
another job, & bless the job I love
because of that bad day. Bless the real
work of learning to listen & absolution
when I don't. Bless being gentle on myself
for not believing these words or receiving these
words though I've said & heard them so many times:
I apologize & I forgive you & I love you very much.
I apologize & I forgive you & I love you very much.
I apologize & I forgive you & I love you very much.

TREE PRAYER

Despite all the chaos from the weather, I am still
on the earth's side. Yes, we have to choose,
one or the other, but it's not between
the bullheaded us or the earth. Instead
it's all of us together or none of us
survive. When I go on walks and pass
large or fallen trees, I place my hand on them
and say a mantra of gratitude. The more
I've done this the more I do this.
Thank you for your beauty.
I like to remember
I am here and I am small.

MY BODY IS A VEHICLE

My body is a vehicle and the drivers rotate.
I mostly toss the keys to the poet I read at first
light, today the older Jim Harrison who doctors
say should no longer drive. He winks his good eye
at me and steers the wheel into a thicket full
of Carolina wren. We've learned to play
the universal game of soul and flesh
and our reward? Still poems about birds.

SCATTERING HER ASHES

We let the indigo bunting choose
on the mountain the rainy morning where
beneath the ledge a waterfall
alive as you were for all our lives until
you weren't and now we carry all
your life passing you
like a peace pipe like phonetic
history that sounded out
the perfect spelling of wonder
and here we are taking the reins
of adulthood stepping through
the time tense boundaries to the edge of
you with the sentinel bunting silent
in respect we open our hands
we give you back to feed the natural
want the animal curiosity
watching the bodydust of you disappear
into the place where sky and mountain meet
that's what you become the space
where birds fly
disappear and return

SOMETIMES I TRY TO SAVE THE WORLD ONLY TO FIND IT'S ALREADY BEEN SAVED

Young girl thirteen but barely
at our table full of books her eyes
full of hunger of knowledge
of recognition she knows
a mirror when she sees a mirror
her mother and little sister three
tables down her eyes fall
on our anthology of southern
queer writers we're in Memphis after
all she asks how much
it costs and I say it's on sale just
for this minute this hour of this day
it's free I speak quickly I whisper
when I say it not knowing
the giants of her life I tell her
to put it in her bag before
her mother and little sister
join us before the little sister points
to the same anthology of queer writers
before the little sister
tells her mother she wants it
before her mother says baby
as long as you are reading
I'll buy you all the books
in the world

BROTHER LISTEN

1

Remembering now how I dreamed
the river was alive   not just alive
but living   long gone then returned
like a first lover with
those pleasures   those shames
dredged from the bottom
all those things we whispered
when no one else was there to hear
all the right and wrong
of who we were
when we thought the world wasn't looking
of who we are
when we think that still

2

It's the summer the river floods our dreams
our waking hours too   as the water rises
state-owned drones fly up and down
recording the levels   recording us
this is a scene from a film we all watched
years ago   if we would have said
that film would come true
who would have believed

3

I have been questioned by that river
hard questions when the truth as I know it
was all I had in answer
having been sworn in
on the book of my life
the book I am still writing   knowing
those in power try to rewrite the story
the poet's job is to stop them   our job:
report what we see
in the camps   in the kitchens
know that when we do
they will make our eyes illegal
our reports unreliable   don't believe me
but it's happening already
and if we ever hold the power
the story we tell must be a story of the truth
both the pleasure and the shame
we must tell all of it

4

The pleasure:
across the street the black orb of a camera
in line with the windows of our new apartment
we walk up fifty stairs   assess what we carry
what's worth it   what is not
the antique furniture abandoned on the ground floor
the vanity   a reflection of the century
the dresser that held the clothing of my family
and then our family   the bedframe
a wedding gift from my great grandparents
to my grandparents in the cold basement
of the house we've left behind
no one can keep everything
the camera   activated by movement
when we forget to close the curtains
when you remember to touch
my legs   lift them on your shoulders
oh weathervane of our living
rooms   I remember the weight of you
in all of them   there was a time
I did keep everything   the portraits
from other walls   other lives
the remnants of seasons I wanted so to touch
when just that wanting was a crime   the lists
of my desires in the books that others wrote
well   I left behind those books
I've walked away from all of it
up the stairs to these windows   awakening
the machine we ignore   there is the luxury
of being here   the luxury of being seen
and the luxury not to care

5

It is in this river of luxury
some by birth can swim   this river
even with injustice carries less injustice
carries less inherited trauma   inherited rage
how steam rises easy from its waters
on the 4th day of July
it doesn't know   why
a father and daughter
would die in it   would die for it
it still believes in every baptism
in sin so easily absolved
a foot-on-the-throat apology
with every patriotic display
red (anger) blue (night) white (well—)
it is an American dream
of a river in an America
dreaming of itself
brother   though I myself have almost drowned
sometimes I am guilty of having this same dream

6

Brother listen   those of us blessed with
knowing safety   those of us at home
in the castles of our own bones
raised with the notion every dream was ours
how are we to know the trickery of that notion
if we don't walk silent into other doors
othered spaces   understand
that every minute
eyes are scanning for some familiar
the nearest exit   a safe bathroom
a stall with a lock   and along the highway
billboards for insurance   billboards for banks
no face a mirror
or when the elevator
opens to men with guns and badges
though they have not come for us
we would swallow down the terror
brother   friend
we know who writes the stories of the laws

7

I am learning
though it has taken 40 years
the othered body's language when
that body's sole purpose
is to survive
but in the body celebrated
complacency is *confederate*
a word that means: *accomplice*   knowledge
only gained when I was silent
enough to understand
(we know who writes the stories of the laws)

8

The warnings go out the levees have breached
though the message is in error
and this night they hold   still
the levees breach in other places
other ways   don't be surprised
we have done this
we have always done this
the violent spectacle   the bombast brutality
the women in cages   groups
walled off with words that make
the human less than human   make us *inmate*
enemy   foreign   our monsters ourselves
waving all the flags we were raised to love or fear
the people on the lists or in the prisons
ask yourself the hard questions
do you trust the system that puts them there
do you trust the system that keeps them there

9

After the flood we face what's left
the drying aftermath of our political opposite
the sand that clings to everything
the shrunken river strange and calm
the trees   their roots exposed
slowly let go of their limbs
their severed blooms spread like
shattered glass across the road
blood diamonds of weather and history
but whose blood   and whose diamonds
this pleasure and this shame

10

I promised you truth:
every morning we cross the river
the quarterly profits grow   we make
more money than ever before   pay less in taxes
talk of buying new shoes   another jacket
we want to ask the woman who wears a blanket her name
a food she loves   *mashed potatoes and gravy*
we want to make her a plate   we will do this   promise
ourselves   we will do this
the later it gets   how careless movements sting
the cigarettes on the ground   the bodies of bees
the people in our lives
who say things so casually   *do as we do here*
you must protect your own   you must learn the language
[you must
love the ruin]
this is America
            this is America ::
flood waters on choking farmland
across industry of incarceration   across industry of illness
whale whose insides are more plastic than whale
            [and you will never forget this]
never forget
these questions begging answers
as if someone were starving ::
my country [my body]:
what are we made of
and when did it happen
and where were we when it did

WHAT I NEED HIM TO SAY

You don't remember my voice, and that's okay.
You have my wallet in the desk beside your bed.
I was your first best friend.

You did use my death. You do.

But, brother, listen.

My death was not trivial to you.
My death was not an act in your play,
or if it was, you were playing yourself.

My death turned off all the lights in the house
and you had to learn to turn them on,
one by one.

In every room I was there.

I know you worked with what you had.

I know you have lived extraordinary moments
standing on my absent shoulders.

I know what you built with my bones.

You built yourself a man.

Forgive yourself for that.

If you need to read those words again, read them again.

(Forgive yourself.)

BUMPER STICKER

It's my brother's 50th birthday today
or it would have been. He's been dead
so long that he's a character in some
book I read or wrote in 8th grade.
He's been dead so long I ought to write
a new book just to see what he'd be like
now as a grown man with a wife and children,
a job he liked or didn't, a bumper sticker
I couldn't stand on the back of his truck.
I want to have a beer with him. I want to
make him laugh. I want to know the way
my life would have gone had I not used
his death to fill the empty places
in my growing body, a tragic cast set
on both of my legs, neither of which
were broken. Oh but I thought they were.

STORM WARNING

An 85-miles-per-hour wall of water
downed power lines this morning. Our old tree
is still standing though many of our neighbors
can't say the same. A few miles over on a nice street
in front of nice houses cars burn in the rain.
The crow and I, we know each other's voices
and send word we survived. Similarly, friends
swap photos of the latest signs of the times.
I still talk to people who've allowed this
to happen, but the conversations
are empty. I don't love them anymore.
I've chosen the crow, the tree, and
our nephew, who turned one yesterday.

BROTHERFUL

Brother, I found photographs of you today. Of us.
How much does a child remember of those first years?
In what I've forgotten, how often were you there?
These photographs say constant. I am drawn to
the ways our bodies were bridges to one another,
your arm against my arm, hand in hand or thigh
pressed to thigh. Brother as reflection, as shadow,
same clothing, same smile, in every photo so much
feeling to witness, to feel. And now so much loss,
something private, a quiet mourning for myself,
for the body more alike to mine than any other body.
These photographs remind me to love you. Brother,
I found you today.
Stay.

ACKNOWLEDGMENTS

Brother Listen (Section 10) / *What Things Cost*

Brothers / *Lovejets: Queer Male Poets on 200 Years of Walt Whitman*

Caretaker of the World / *Chiron Review*

Electricity / *Burning House Press*

Lineage (Family) / *The Container Project* & *Mollyhouse*

Lineage (Kisses) / Correspondence from Ian Young

They Say the Music You Hear at Fourteen Is the Music of Your Life / *Lovejets: Queer Male Poets on 200 Years of Walt Whitman*

Tree Prayer / *Chiron Review*

The Wild / *Oxford American*

The title of this book is credited to my friend Raymond Luczak.

The quoted poem in "You Are Not Here" is "Immortality" by Clare Harner.

Forever gratitude to Seth Pennington for his eyes, for his talent, for his hands, for his heart, and for this family he gifted me.

ABOUT THE POET

Bryan Borland is founding publisher of Sibling Rivalry Press. He lives in Arkansas with his husband, Seth Pennington. (www.bryanborland.com)

OTHER WORK

Crow in the Desert (Queer Punk Collective, 2025)

Tourist (Sibling Rivalry Press, 2018)

DIG (Stillhouse Press, 2016); a finalist for the Lambda Literary Award in Gay Poetry and a Stonewall Honor Book in Literature as selected by the American Library Association

Less Fortunate Pirates (Sibling Rivalry Press, 2012)

My Life as Adam (Sibling Rivalry Press, 2010)

ABOUT THE PRESS

Sibling Rivalry Press is an independent press based in North Little Rock, Arkansas. It is a sponsored project of Fractured Atlas, a nonprofit arts service organization. Contributions to support the operations of Sibling Rivalry Press are tax-deductible to the extent permitted by law, and your donations will directly assist in the publication of work that disturbs and enraptures. To contribute to the publication of more books like this one, please visit our website and click *donate*.

www.ingramcontent.com/pod-product-compliance
Lightning Source LLC
Chambersburg PA
CBHW020217090426
42734CB00008B/1112